The Juice Bar Business Plan

Discover How to Start a Successful Juice Bar Business

by Simone Armstrong

Table of Contents

Introduction 1

Chapter 1: Crafting a Solid Business Plan 7

Chapter 2: Conducting In-Depth Market Research . 11

Chapter 3: It's All in the Name 17

Chapter 4: Location, Location, Location 21

Chapter 5: Getting Licensed 25

Chapter 6: Equipment You Will Need 29

Chapter 7: The Key to Making Sales 35

Conclusion 39

Introduction

Nowadays, a lot of folks are making the effort to lead healthier lifestyles. More than ever, people are becoming conscious of their health and over all well-being. People are taking up sports and exercise, watching their weight, and staying away from processed foods and harmful ingredients. Consequently, this movement has created a market for products that promote healthy living.

Delightful and flavorful concoctions made from unprocessed, all-natural ingredients have become one of the top-selling "healthy-lifestyle" products. Health-conscious consumers adore delicious drinks made from fresh fruits, vegetables, or a combination of both. Because of this growing and eager market, starting a juice bar business can prove to be a very appealing and profitable business venture.

What does it take to open your own juice bar? Just like in any kind of business, research and careful planning are all necessary to guarantee a successful startup. On top of that, there are numerous things that one needs to know to make sure an entrepreneur is ready for the challenges of starting a juice bar business.

Interested in opening a juice bar? Then this book is for you. We have outlined the step-by-step process of starting this kind of business from start to success. We will present the nuts and bolts of the whole juice bar business. After reading this book, you will see that there is no mystery and that anyone who has what it takes can start his or her very own juice bar business.

© Copyright 2014 by Miafn LLC - All rights reserved.

This document is geared towards providing reliable information in regards to the topic and issue covered. The publication is sold with the idea that the publisher is not required to render accounting, officially permitted, or otherwise, qualified services. If advice is necessary, legal or professional, a practiced individual in the profession should be ordered.

- From a Declaration of Principles which was accepted and approved equally by a Committee of the American Bar Association and a Committee of Publishers and Associations.

In no way is it legal to reproduce, duplicate, or transmit any part of this document in either electronic means or in printed format. Recording of this publication is strictly prohibited and any storage of this document is not allowed unless with written permission from the publisher. All rights reserved.

The information provided herein is stated to be truthful and consistent, in that any liability, in terms of inattention or otherwise, by any usage or abuse of any policies, processes, or directions contained within is solely and completely the responsibility of the recipient reader. Under no circumstances will any legal responsibility or blame be held against the publisher for any reparation, damages, or monetary loss due to the information herein, either directly or indirectly.

Respective authors own all copyrights not held by the publisher.

The information herein is offered for informational purposes solely, and is universal as so. The presentation of the information is without contract or any type of guarantee assurance.

The trademarks that are used are without any consent, and the publication of the trademark is without permission or backing by the trademark owner. All trademarks and brands within this book are for clarifying purposes only and are the owned by the owners themselves, not affiliated with this document.

Chapter 1: Crafting a Solid Business Plan

The business plan is one of the most essential first steps in starting any kind of business. It is unfortunate that not many young entrepreneurs take the time and effort to create a viable and sound business plan. Creating a business plan is the very first step in starting a juice bar business.

If you haven't done one yet, block off time as soon as possible to start making one. Do an initial draft and then work on it until you have a feasible business plan that will save you a lot of time, money, and effort when you actually launch your business. The purpose of creating a business plan is for you to plan every detail of your business venture. By doing so, expenses can be reduced and the chances of success can be increased. A lot of new startup businesses fail due to factors that could have been anticipated and considered in a thorough business plan. Without a sound business plan, it's like going to war where you have no idea what going to happen. With a carefully prepared business plan, you don't know what will happen but at least you are prepared, not for everything but at least some things that might come your way.

Your business plan should include detailed information on the product, the kind of fruits you will make juice from, the types of blends or flavors you will offer, etc. It should describe your plans in relation to the findings in your market study: the profile of your target customers, competition, location, vendors, equipment, staff, and marketing. It should also include your plans for funding and at least a three-year analysis of operating expenses and profit projections. The more comprehensive your business plan, the better.

The business plan should be a work in progress. Once you come up with one, it doesn't mean that you're done with it. Review your business plan every so often. Carefully go over it and painstakingly check for any weakness. Keep in mind that your business plan should be like a fortress. If you can poke holes at this fortress, it means that your business plan is still a long way to becoming perfect. A sound business plan must cover everything from the smallest detail to the most complicated part of your business operation.

Consult with an expert and get professional advice, if necessary. Do your own research and learn as much as you can about the juice bar business. If you come across aspects of the business that you are not yet familiar with, such as management, accounting, operations, marketing etc., don't be afraid to reach out to people that possess knowledge and experience about these.

Present your business plan to a bank. It will be reviewed in detail and if the bank experts thinks that your proposal is solid and the plan is likely to succeed, they can offer to fund it.

Don't rush off and open a juice business that you are not prepared for. Be patient and take your time in the planning phase. While a number of new entrepreneurs might miss the importance of creating a viable business plan, experienced businesspeople understand how a well-prepared business plan can affect your chances of success. The next chapters will provide detailed information about what your juice bar business plan should include.

Chapter 2: Conducting In-Depth Market Research

Market research is essential in creating a business plan. Although the juice bar business is quite popular in many parts of the globe, certain juices may not be a hit in some areas due to certain factors. Studying the market beforehand, regardless of the kind of business, allows the entrepreneur to obtain useful information about the market, its size, and its needs. A market study helps pin-point and analyze the customers' needs and preferences.

Among the first questions you need to answer is whether you'll have customers or not. And if you do have customers, are there enough of them to make your business profitable? In doing a thorough market research for your juice bar business, you will also be able to study the demand for juice, identify your target customers, know the kind of juice that customers prefer, and gain information about the competing businesses.

Franchise or Start from Scratch?

When starting a juice bar business you have two options: buy into a franchise or start a new juice bar business. Both of these methods have their advantages and disadvantages. Your market research will be able to provide you all the information that you need so that you can decide which option to take.

Among the advantages of buying into a juice bar franchise include guaranteed customers – people who are already patrons of the established juice bar. In addition, when you buy into a franchise, you also get the brand name and the good reputation that goes with it, plus, you have access to support and resources from the mother company. But if you are planning on developing your own juice recipes and you are bent on creating a certain look for your store, then a franchise may not be for you. Don't forget the costly franchise fees, too. If you are more interested in buying into a franchise, then start getting in contact with the juice bar companies operating in your area and make your inquiries.

On the other hand, when you start an independent juice bar, you have full control of everything from the juice recipes, prices, store décor, and everything else. And you'll get a chance to attract and build your own customers, create a good reputation, and do all things independently. However, you will likely need to work harder to get your target customers to try your products as a brand new name as opposed to an established franchise.

Types of Juice Bars

There are two kinds of juice bars and both are popular among health enthusiasts.

Mobile

Mobile juice bars are exactly that – mobile! That means your products are actually more accessible to potential customers. People on-the-go can easily buy from you. Mobile juice bars can either be parked in locations such as the entrance of a school or a fitness center, or you can drive it around neighborhoods to reach more health-conscious consumers! The great thing about a mobile juice bar is that you can bring it to all kinds of public events such as festivals, sports events, outdoor concerts, and so on.

Fixed

The juice bar is stationed in one location and operates in a restaurant or café style. Customers can sit and drink their beverages leisurely. The juice bar can also be a place where people can just hang around while sipping their nutritious and delicious drinks.

Studying the Competition

In any kind of business, it is unwise to totally ignore the competition. In fact, it is advisable to pay close attention to your competitors. This is the best way to maintain your business' competitiveness. If your competition is either failing or succeeding, you have to know why. Do a research on the juice bars operating in your area and learn as much as you can about the products or services that they are offering their customers. With this information, you can modify and improve your own juice bar business and at the same time, increase your chances of success.

Chapter 3: It's All in the Name

There are so many possibilities when it comes to naming your juice bar business. Choosing a name will need careful consideration. Remember that the name you choose will greatly affect your product's marketability and ultimately, your business' success.

Many successful juice bar businesses have catchy names and the beverages they offer have names that are equally striking. When naming your juice bar business, it's important that you select a name that is unique but something that people can easily remember.

Naming Your Juice Bar

- **Keep it short.**

A maximum of three words should be the rule when picking out a name for your business. More than that, your brand name becomes a mouthful and customers will have a hard time saying it. Short names are easy to recall. You wouldn't want your customers to always call you 'that new juice bar' or 'that juice place by the corner'. Your goal is to have your customers remember you by name.

- **Keep it simple.**

Depending on your target market, name your juice bar business something that your customers can easily relate to. For instance, if your target market is mostly Americans, don't choose a French name or some fancy Italian name for your business. Your customers should be able to relate to your name and should easily understand what it is that you are selling.

- **Make it yours.**

Whatever name you choose for your juice bar business, make sure that it has a special meaning to you. Because with the numerous juice bar businesses today, it's possible that another business is already using the generic name that you came up with. Be sure to check that your business name is unique and that no other company goes by it.

Naming Your Products

It's a whole new ball game when it comes to naming your products. This time you would like to stand out among your competitors. Put a lot of thought in naming your juice recipes because eventually, your store will be known for the beverages that you serve. Don't just go by the usual 'Mango Juice', 'Strawberry Smoothie' or 'Banana and Vanilla Shake'. Be creative and come up with special names for your drinks. It makes your products notable and can become part of your company's branding. In your market research, study what your competitors are naming their products. This way, you can get an idea and you can avoid using the same names for your beverages. You can also check time and again in case there are trademark conflicts between you and the competition.

Chapter 4: Location, Location, Location

Location is vital to the success of your business. The selection of the ideal location of your juice bar should get a significant amount of your time and energy. You won't be making the profit that you're supposed to, even if you got everything right, if your customers just can't get to your product.

Location is everything when it comes to a juice bar business. When looking for the right spot for selling your nutritious drinks, your initial consideration should be your target customers. Your juice products can be bought by everyone but you are mostly promoting health drinks so it's best if you can set up your store near a fitness center, a gym, or a sports club. High traffic areas like a shopping mall, a school, or a park are also good locations for your business.

When selecting the location for your juice bar business, check out the neighborhood first. What establishments are operating in the surrounding area? A good spot would be near restaurants, cafes, and other food businesses. It's also advantageous to be in the same block as your competitor. You can watch each other and customers will be swarming the area.

If you have opted for a mobile juice bar, then you can just move all around your zone, selecting stations where you can get the most customers. With a mobile juice bar, you can drive to a flea market, fair, carnival, festival, concert, and many other outdoor events. If you are going for the fixed store, you should also consider setting up booths in all kinds of places as these can be very great venues to sell your healthful drinks.

Once you have set up your store, you should also look into bottling your juices. That way, you can have your products sold at grocery stores, delis, cafes, restaurants, and fitness centers. The possibilities are endless when it comes to venues for selling your fruit juices.

Chapter 5: Getting Licensed

The next step is to acquire all required permits and licenses so that you can operate your juice bar business legally. There are certain permits and licenses that all food-related businesses must obtain before they can start serving food and drinks to customers.

Vendor License

A vendor license is a standard requirement for any person who wishes to make profit by selling his or her product. Like all businesses, juice bar owners are also required to obtain one before they can offer their beverages to the public. It is advisable that you consult with your State's local office and learn more about the guidelines for securing a vendor license in your area. They can tell you what type of vendor license you need to apply for depending on the type of juice bar you plan to open.

Health Permit

Local governments require all food establishments to obtain a health permit. This will ensure that all food and drinks sold to the public are clean and safe. Juice bar owners need to apply for this permit. There is a process that the local health department needs to follow before releasing the health permit to the juice bar owner. First, the store will be visited and thoroughly inspected by health department representatives. They will make sure that your store passes all the sanitary requirements and that the owner is following all health and safety regulations. The number of visits and inspections to your store is subject to the standards set by the local health department. This is not the time to worry or to feel discouraged. Instead, every entrepreneur must use this chance to improve his or her store until it passes the inspections. In case a store fails the scrutiny, the owner will be given a period to address the concerns and will undergo the same process again.

Zoning Permit

Juice bars set up in a fixed location need to apply for a zoning permit. Zoning permits are required for all building constructions and remodeling. You won't need this permit if you chose to operate a mobile juice bar. Nevertheless, the regulations on acquiring zoning permits can vary per locality so just to be on the safe side, inquire about it from your local government office.

General Business Licenses and Permits

Entrepreneurs planning on opening a juice bar are also required to obtain other general business permits and licenses. Among these include the Sales and Use Tax License and the license to operate a business as sole proprietorship, partnership, or corporation. Talk to someone from the local government office and they will be willing to guide you in securing all the necessary permits and licenses that you need in order to open your juice bar business.

Chapter 6: Equipment You Will Need

Part of knowing how to run a juice bar business is knowing the different equipment needed in its day to day operations. But it's not just about buying all the equipment being sold. You have to study which specific ones are best to use for your particular business.

Your juice bar equipment need not be the most expensive. However, it needs to be the most efficient. So when buying your equipment, be sure to choose each tool carefully, weighing cost and efficiency. As with most purchases, buying cheap may save you money now but will cost your double later on.

To get you started, here is a list of the equipment that you'll need in opening a juice bar.

Blenders

You might want to buy at least a couple of heavy-duty, commercial blenders. There are various brands that you can choose from. Do some research on what specific brands offer. Also, look into what your competitors are using. If you don't have much experience with the juice business yet, it's best to go with the brand of blenders that have already been tried-and-tested or are used by professionals. You might want to look for commercial blenders that have the following features: efficient design, made from durable materials, has a comprehensive warranty that includes repairs of parts, and sound reduction hoods.

Juicers

Blenders and juicers are the heart of your juice business. These are your main equipment so make sure that you invest in high-quality blenders and juicers. Here are the three types of juicers that you can use in running your juice bar business.

- **Centrifugal Juicers**

This type of juicer is quite affordable compared to the other types. Its motors work fast, running between 3,000RPM to 14,000RPM. The centrifugal juicers are considered as one of the fastest juicers in the market today. This type of juicer is recommended for startup juice bar businesses.

- **Masticating Juicers**

This type of juicer uses single gear. Many juice bar owners prefer this type of juicer due to its ability to crush fruits, vegetables, and other natural ingredients slowly and methodically. Due to this process, the juice produced is notably higher in nutritional value. Moreover, this juicer does not make a lot of noise.

- **Triturating Juicers**

Considered the top dog of juicers, this type of juicer utilizes twin gears when extracting healthful juices. This is the best juicer for creating nutritional drinks as it uses a gentle, relaxed process that allows less oxidation in the ingredients. This is the best type of juicer for organic juices.

Refrigeration

Since the main ingredients for your health beverages are made from produce, you'll need to invest in a walk-in refrigerator. Here is where you'll keep all your fruits and vegetable fresh. If you have a mobile juice bar, then a cooler or a small refrigerator will work just fine. Some fruits and vegetables keep better if stored in room temperature, so make provisions for a pantry too.

Ice Machine

Many customers prefer cool drinks especially in the warm weather. And if you are planning on doing smoothies too, then an ice machine is necessary. Look into the types of ice machines available in the market and get one that suits your needs. A cubed ice machine can be a good investment, but you might like the flaked ice machine better as it produces smooth ice that is best for smoothies.

Counters, Sinks, Work Station

Prepare an area where you and your staff can prepare the ingredients. There should also be a separate juicing station and a place to wash hands and utensils. Put in sinks for the prep area, juicing station, and washing area.

Dishwasher

If you're planning on a big juice bar, then invest in an under-the-counter dishwasher. This will help keep your blenders and juicers clean. The cleaning time is faster too. But if you plan on a small juice bar, then a sink for washing is recommended.

Preparation Tools and Equipment

Of course, you need to invest in other utensils that you would normally use in a kitchen.

- Knives
- Peelers
- Chopping boards
- Portion scales
- Measuring cups
- Measuring Spoons

Point of Sale System

Almost all food businesses use a point of sale system as it makes business transactions more efficient. You, too, have to select a good POS system for your juice bar. It will help you in the day-to-day management of your business.

Chapter 7: The Key to Making Sales

Marketing your name and your products is one of the best ways to help your profit. The more people know about your business and what you're offering to consumers, the higher your profit will be.

Marketing and Advertising

In your business plan, you made a study about the best ways to market your product. There should also be funds that are specifically allotted for this purpose. Your market research can help you identify the best ways to let your customer know about your juice bar company and the drinks that you're offering. TV, radio, and newspaper ads are the most common ways to advertise your business but you can also try advertising in newsletters, pamphlets, and other smaller publications such as the local college paper. Social media is probably the most powerful tool in marketing today so remember to use you social network to make your product known.

Don't be afraid to use gimmicks to advertise your products. For instance, you can give free drinks to customers who complete a 'purchase card' or 'frequency card'. Depending on your profit margins, you can offer to give a free drink for every ten or so drinks that they buy. Offer all sorts of promos and give discounts to your loyal customers. They will love coming back to your store. You should also put up posters or ads of your juice bar inside fitness centers, gyms, and sports clubs. Make deals with the management so that they can sell your health drinks to their patrons in exchange for advertising their business in your own store.

Creating Your Trademark

By now, you are aware that there are a number of competitors in your area. How can you stand out from the pack? The answer is to create your trademark. Come up with clever names for your drinks. But more than catchy names, you need to create unique juice recipes and offer delicious, healthful drinks that your customers can only find in your store and nowhere else. When you have a trademark drink or trademark menu, your customers will remember your store better and you'll be able to build a strong reputation.

Diversify

While it's true that your focus is in making your juice products be known, it does not hurt to diversify in your business. That's the beauty of selling beverages! You can pair it with snacks and meals. But make sure that you stick to the theme of your business which is healthy products. A salad bar that offers healthy salads can be a great partner of your nutritious drinks. You might also consider creating healthy menus that feature your fruit and vegetable drinks for beverages.

Conclusion

If you are a regular customer of juice bars in your area and you just can't get enough of fruit juices, vegetable juices, smoothies, and organic shakes, then why not open your own juice bar? If you are health-conscious and you know many other like-minded individuals out there, what better way to support a healthy lifestyle than to promote and sell healthful drinks?

The juice bar business has been around for a long time. Juice is sold here, there, and everywhere. However, with the awareness for health and the increasing desire of people to live healthier lifestyles, the ordinary fruit juice has been reinvented into a popular, health drink. And the best thing about these healthy drinks is the fact that they are delicious! Kids, teens, and adults can enjoy nutritious vegetable juices without the icky feeling. With the use of modern equipment and the creation of ingenious recipes, vegetable juices have become appealing drinks. Now, people can enjoy a drink that is not only delicious but also nutritious.

Starting a juice bar business today is one of the more promising, and profitable ventures that health-buffs can look into. People like juices, shakes, and smoothies. Now that people are opting for a healthier lifestyle, a juice bar that sells healthy and flavorful beverages is the perfect opportunity to fill a need, give value and make a profit.

Finally, I'd like to thank you for purchasing this book! If you enjoyed it or found it helpful, I'd greatly appreciate it if you'd take a moment to leave a review on Amazon. Thank you!

Made in the USA
Middletown, DE
27 December 2018